PRIMARY SOURCES OF POLITICAL SYSTEMS™

DEMOCRACY
A PRIMARY SOURCE ANALYSIS

BILL STITES

rosen central
Primary Source™

The Rosen Publishing Group, Inc., New York

Published in 2005 by The Rosen Publishing Group, Inc.
29 East 21st Street, New York, NY 10010

Copyright © 2005 by The Rosen Publishing Group, Inc.

First Edition

Library of Congress Cataloging-in-Publication Data

Stites, Bill.
Democracy : a primary source analysis / Bill Stites. — 1st ed.
    p. cm. — (Primary sources of political systems)
Includes bibliographical references (p.   ) and index.
Contents: A long time ago—A new birth of democracy—The American experiment—Elements of Democracy—Democracy's growing pains.
ISBN 0-8239-4518-9 (library binding)
1. Democracy—United States—History—Sources—Juvenile literature. 2. Democracy—History—Sources—Juvenile literature. [1. Democracy. 2. World politics.]
I. Title. II. Series.
JK1726.S75 2003
321.8—dc22

                                                                    2003015895

Manufactured in the United States of America

On the cover: *The Declaration of Independence*, an 1819 painting by John Trumbull, depicts the presentation of the Declaration of Independence to John Hancock, president of the Continental Congress from May 1775 to October 1777.

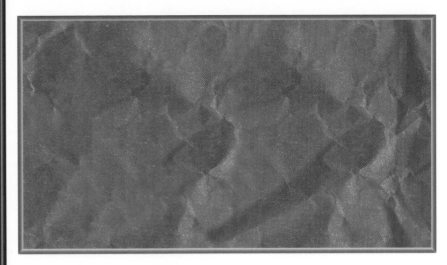

CONTENTS

INTRODUCTION

O ver the centuries, democracy has meant many things to many people. The word "democracy" comes from the ancient Greeks, who are believed to have been the first people to establish a formal democratic government. Yet much about the way the Greeks did things seems very undemocratic to us today. On paper, every citizen of Athens had the right to vote. But the Greeks used the word "citizen" very differently than we do. Most of the people living in Athens were not citizens. Women could not be citizens. Neither could slaves. Neither could anyone who didn't own property. Nowadays, no one would consider such a country to be a democracy. Yet, only 100 years ago, women in America couldn't vote either. And even though black men had the right, they were usually prevented from voting in the South.

So much has changed in such a relatively short time. Today, no one would seriously suggest that a country could exclude more than half of its population from voting and still be considered a democracy. But there have been times when it seemed perfectly normal. So the meaning of democracy has evolved and will probably continue to change.

This photograph shows a large pressroom full of journalists watching a presidential debate between Vice President Al Gore and Texas governor George W. Bush on October 3, 2000. The debate was held at the University of Massachusetts in Boston.

Democracy really means equality. In a democracy, everyone's opinion should count equally. Realistically speaking, complete democracy has never been achieved. And it may never be. But it has long been a goal and an instinct of man. For example, a tribe of hunters and gatherers could never have survived without each person contributing his or her skills. Everyone had to share if anyone was to survive. In a crude way, that is democracy. Tribes and villages predate established government. Before there was government, there was still democracy.

Democracy, in some form, has always been a part of human life. But only in the last few centuries has it spread to the largest governments around the world. And only very recently has it become widely regarded as the ideal way to run a country. More people today enjoy the benefits of democracy than in any other period in history. However, nowhere is democracy perfect. There is still much work to be done.

CHAPTER ONE

A LONG TIME AGO

The story of democracy begins in ancient Greece. Far inland from the coasts, among the rolling hills of the Greek countryside, the first experiments in formal democracy took place.

Ancient Greece was not a single country. There were more than 1,500 distinct city-states sprawling across the land. Each had its own government, completely separate from its neighbors. And each of them had a different kind of government.

The Greek people had a passion for government. They enjoyed tinkering with it, trying new things, and seeing what worked and what didn't. The

This detail from Raphael's *School of Athens* portrays Plato *(left)* and Aristotle having a conversation. Both Greek philosophers viewed democracy as the worst type of government.

city-states borrowed ideas and methods from one another. The English word "politics" comes from the Greek word *polis*, for city-state. Many of our other political words also come from Greek.

There were many different types of government at work in Greece. The ancient Greeks are famous for having developed democracy. But democracies were actually rare. Only two of the city-states gave democracy a serious try: Athens and Sparta. And neither one lasted for long. In fact, the major Greek philosophers agreed that democracy was the worst form of government. Until very recently, most people in history would have agreed with them.

Athenian Democracy

The Greeks understood democracy very differently than has any society since. "Democracy" is a combination of two Greek words, meaning "people" and "rule." The Greeks took it to mean exactly that. What we practice today is called representative democracy. That means we elect representatives to govern for us. Such ideas would have been alien to the Greeks. To them, democracy meant that every single citizen participated in running the city-state.

But not every resident was a citizen. Women could not be citizens. Slavery was legal, and slaves couldn't be citizens. Neither could any-one who didn't own land. Even a person whose family had been in a city-state for fewer than three generations could not be a citizen.

In most democracies today, every adult citizen can vote. But very few people ever have a hand in running their government. In ancient Greece, very few people could vote, but all those who did could play a direct role in their government.

These are the ruins of the speaker's platform at the Pnyx, the place where the Athenian Assembly met to discuss proposals and announce decrees. Historians often refer to it as the birthplace of democracy. In theory, all the citizens of Athens had the right to speak. However, it is likely that wealthy leaders dominated the sessions of the Assembly.

The main governmental body in Athens was called the Assembly. All of the important decisions about running the city-state were made by it. The Assembly was huge: every citizen of Athens was a member. That meant up to 45,000 people could vote on each proposed bill. The Athenians liked to involve as many people as possible in their government. Six thousand people had to be present before a meeting of the Assembly could even begin. Athenian juries typically had 501 jurors.

The Council of 500

Athens expected a lot from its citizens. The Assembly met forty times a year, and every citizen had to attend regularly. But the Assembly couldn't handle all of the city-state's business because some people had to work full-time. Thus, there was a smaller group that met more often. It was called the Council of 500. It drafted the legislation that the Assembly voted on.

The 500 members of the council weren't elected. They were selected by lot, which means that names were drawn at random. Every citizen had an equal chance of being picked. There were also strict term limits. No one could serve on the council for more than two years. As a result, more than 40 percent of the citizens of Athens held office during their lives. Accordingly, more than 40 percent of the people in the Assembly had a firsthand understanding of how the government worked. The Athenians attempted to let every citizen help govern in as many ways as possible. They thought that the more involved a citizen was, the more wisely he would vote—and that would strengthen the democracy.

The Athenians felt that the citizens of a city-state had to share the work of governing. If they didn't, the government would not serve everyone's interests. However, by excluding women and other large groups of people from the government, the Assembly never took those people's issues and interests seriously. By preventing them from participating in the democracy, the Assembly silenced their voices. The Greeks felt strongly that every citizen had to have an equal voice in order for the democracy to be fair. But not every person's voice was

Clay tablets such as the one pictured here were used as juror identification cards in the Athenian court. This tablet includes the juror's name, his father's name, and his village. Athenian juries wielded great power. Their decisions were final. They ruled on all types of cases, including those determining the constitutionality of laws passed by the Assembly.

equal. So corruption and injustice were a fact of life. The citizens were generally treated very well by the government. But the noncitizens were not.

Civil Rights and the Death of Socrates

Another unusual aspect of the Greek democracies was that it never occurred to the Greeks that individuals should have rights. The way they saw it, the government was nothing more than the will of the citizens. So there was no reason why people would need civil rights

After being sentenced to death, Socrates chose to die by drinking poison. In this 1787 painting by Jacques-Louis David, Socrates continues to instruct his students even as he reaches for the cup of poison. He remains energetic and in control, while his students appear dejected by his imminent death. The painting is entitled *The Death of Socrates*.

to protect them from the government. It was a nice idea. But it resulted in some terrible mistakes.

The great philosopher Socrates was sentenced to death for blasphemy by the Assembly. Socrates knew he'd been falsely accused. However, he believed so strongly in democracy that he chose to respect his countrymen's wishes and poison himself. His student Plato never forgave the Assembly for his teacher's death. He always harbored a great distrust of democracy. Plato's writings and those

SPARTAN DEMOCRACY

Athens is the better known of the ancient Greek democracies. But, before it, there was another city-state that gave democracy a try. It was called Sparta.

The Spartans were in some ways very advanced for their time. They had public education for the sons and daughters of their citizens. They treated their citizens as equals in every way. In Sparta, though, even fewer people could be citizens than in Athens.

The Spartans were militaristic. They defeated several nearby societies in battle and claimed their lands. The people they conquered outnumbered the native Spartans ten to one. But the Spartans never extended democracy to them. Only native Spartan men could be citizens.

The Spartans had to maintain a very strong army to keep their subjects in line. Spartan boys began training for the army at age seven. They were required to serve in the army until they turned thirty. They did not become citizens until their army service had been completed.

If the Spartans had included the people they conquered in their democracy, they may not have needed to organize their society around their military. Freed from that obligation, perhaps they would have excelled in art and philosophy the way the Athenians did.

of his student Aristotle criticized democracy. These works were widely read in Europe for thousands of years after they were written. They influenced European thought for centuries.

The Legacy of Ancient Greece

The brief period in which democracy flourished in ancient Greece left us with some of the greatest writing the world has ever seen. The playwrights and philosophers of Athens are still widely read today.

Unfortunately, Athenian democracy didn't last. Invading armies from Sparta eventually conquered Athens in 404 BC. When they did, democracy ended. But Plato's and Aristotle's histories remained.

Ironically, although Plato and Aristotle were critical of democracy, their accounts of the political system intrigued people anyway. Eventually, some Europeans began to wonder if the Greeks had been on to something. By then, Europe was firmly under the control of its kings and queens. Although Europe would witness a number of movements advocating a greater role for representative bodies in government between the thirteenth and seventeenth centuries, it was difficult for democracy to gain a foothold. However, the founding of the United States in the late eighteenth century and its subsequent rise to global power led to the spread of democracy around the world.

CHAPTER TWO

A NEW BIRTH OF DEMOCRACY

THOMAS JEFFERSON.
Third President of the United States.

F or 2,000 years after the fall of Athens, no Western nation invested its power in the democratic method. Monarchy was the rule of Europe. For centuries, royal families had promoted the theory of the divine right of kings. They claimed it was God's will that they rule. Otherwise, the argument went, why would they be ruling? With the church's help, royalty kept an iron grip on power for a long, long time.

An early challenge to this royal claim surfaced in thirteenth-century England. In 1215, a group of barons led an armed rebellion against King John. They were protesting against high taxes, the

Thomas Jefferson was the principal author of the American Declaration of Independence. He wrote it when he was only thirty-three years old.

After agreeing to his barons' demands, King John authorized that handwritten copies of the Magna Carta be prepared and read throughout England. One of those copies, bearing his seal, is pictured here. Refer to page 56 for a partial transcription of the Magna Carta.

king's ruthless punishment of those who could not or did not pay, and what they considered other abuses of royal power. After capturing London, the barons forced the king into signing a document that limited the power of the king and his heirs and guaranteed certain civil and political liberties. This document became known as the Magna Carta, or great charter. However, once the hostilities were over, King John felt entitled to break the charter to which he had agreed under pressure. Fifty years later, the English Parliament came into existence during a rebellion against John's son, King Henry III.

In the early 1600s, royalty's grip on power began to loosen. The growth of the middle class made it harder for monarchs to keep their subjects in line. The Catholic Church broke up into many factions, reducing its power. In addition, philosophers such as John Locke, Jean-Jacques Rousseau, and Thomas Hobbes questioned the nature of government. In England in 1688, after a protracted dispute, Parliament deposed King James II and replaced him with King William III and Queen Mary II. More

This stone carving portrays the Archbishop of Canterbury Stephen Langton handing the Magna Carta to King John for his seal in the presence of a couple of barons. The carving is situated on the pulpit at the National Cathedral in Washington, D.C., in recognition of the influence of the Magna Carta on American democracy.

important, Parliament asserted its supremacy over the monarchy and forever limited its power, rendering it mostly symbolic.

As this happened, people were settling in the colonies in America. Many of them were victims of religious persecution. They braved the long trip to America to find a place where they could worship freely. Unlike anyplace else, the ideals of freedom and independence were always crucial parts of the American character.

At first, England, France, Spain, and other countries controlled parts of America's eastern coast. The only way colonists could communicate with their mother countries was by sending messages by ship. But it took a long time to receive an answer. So the colonists developed local governments to handle day-to-day matters. After a while, some of the colonists began to question why they should answer to a country across the ocean.

The Battle for Democracy

By the late 1700s, the situation between England and the colonies had gotten antagonistic. War between the colonial government and its subjects became inevitable. This was not the first time such a thing had happened. But it would be the first time that the men behind a revolution would seek democracy as their remedy.

George Washington, Thomas Jefferson, and the other architects of the revolution were wealthy. If America had had a royal class, they certainly would have been part of it. They were also scholars. They had read Locke and Rousseau. They had studied the ancient Greeks. They had seen firsthand how religious freedom had benefitted American society. And they began to think about extending that freedom in other ways.

In 1774, representatives from twelve of the thirteen colonies met in Philadelphia. They called the meeting the Continental Congress. Almost immediately, they issued a list of grievances they had with their king, George III, and the English Parliament. By 1775, the king had not yet responded to their demands. So the Continental Congress met again. This time, they would develop a plan to unify the colonies.

Words That Shocked the World

By July 1776, the colonists had lost all hope that they could resolve their problems with England. They decided it was time to formally separate from England. With that goal, the colonies sent delegates to a meeting in Philadelphia to write another statement. Thomas Jefferson was regarded as the best writer among them, so he was made the head of the committee. He was to be the primary author of the Declaration of Independence.

Jefferson had been given a task no one before him had ever undertaken. Not only did he have to announce the birth of a democracy, but he also had to justify democracy to the world. He spent about two weeks drafting the declaration. The document he created was as revolutionary as any ever set to paper.

This is the beginning of the second paragraph of the Declaration of Independence:

> We hold these truths to be self-evident, that all men are created equal, that they are endowed by their Creator with certain unalienable Rights, that among these are Life, Liberty and the pursuit of Happiness.

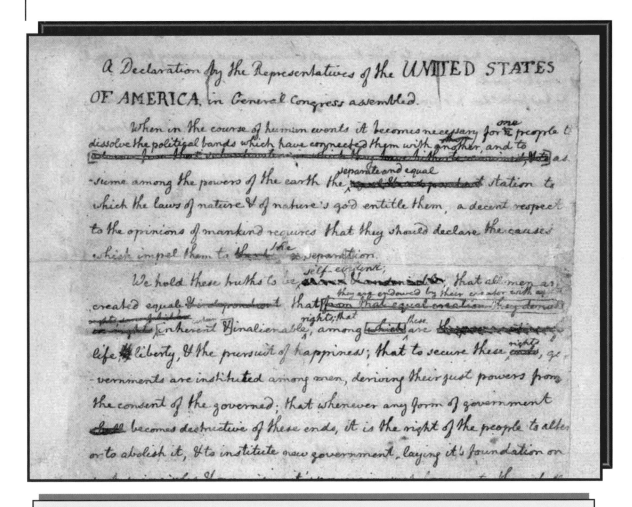

This is a page from Jefferson's original rough draft of the Declaration of Independence. The revisions that appear above the crossed-out passages were made by John Adams and Benjamin Franklin. The final document was adopted by Congress on July 4, 1776. Refer to page 56 for a partial transcription of the Declaration of Independence.

There is no precedent for what he did with those words. There was no country on earth at the time that sought to guarantee the liberty of individuals. But Jefferson had the courage to stand up and announce that all humans shared certain rights, which no government could take away from them. He was even bold enough to say that this was so clear as to be "self-evident." That seems natural to most of us today, but at the time it shocked the world. He may have thought the things he said were obvious. But there were a lot of people at the time who disagreed with him.

The Declaration of Independence is unique because it's not a political document. It is not a constitution. It is a statement of beliefs. Jefferson had no idea when he wrote it what form democracy in America would take. But he set a standard for what it should be, and the country has been working toward that ever since. The government he envisioned would be founded on a noble principle. He set out an ideal of America as a place that would protect the rights of all its citizens. In one sentence, Jefferson shook the institution of monarchy to its core.

The declaration continues:

> That to secure these rights, Governments are instituted among Men, deriving their just powers from the consent of the governed.

The phrase "consent of the governed" comes from John Locke. Those words were very threatening to the people in power at the time. They represented a complete disregard for the theory of divine right. To Locke, the citizens wielded the real power. Their rulers could rule them only if they allowed themselves to be ruled. By implying that a people could take away their consent to be governed, his words inherently justified revolution.

And so, Jefferson followed them by announcing one:

> That whenever any Form of Government becomes destructive of these ends, it is the Right of the People to alter or abolish it, and

This engraving by Edward Savage is entitled *Congress Voting the Declaration of Independence*. It was created around 1776. In it, Thomas Jefferson lays the declaration on the table at right, while other members of the Continental Congress look on.

to institute new Government, laying its foundation on such principles and organizing its powers in such form, as to them shall seem most likely to effect their Safety and Prudence.

That sentence, like the one before it, overturned a centuries-old concept of government. Rather than a nation's citizens being completely subjugated to an absolute monarch appointed by God, government existed to serve them and was theirs to decide.

THE IROQUOIS DEMOCRACY

America's democracy wasn't influenced only by European cultures. It's hard to believe that America's government was in part inspired by the political system of the Iroquois when one considers how terribly the United States treated these Native American people over the centuries.

The Iroquois had a democratic government centuries before the first European settlers arrived. Passing their rules and laws down orally, they had developed a sophisticated democracy even before they discovered written language. They called their constitution the Great Binding Law. It united five nations of Native American people. It also lasted longer than any other democracy ever has.

The Great Binding Law created a single governmental body for all the Iroquois called the Great Council. Each nation was equally represented. The women of each tribe selected the representatives to the Great Council.

There is no doubt that the framers of the U.S. Constitution admired the Iroquois system. They may have even modeled some aspects of their democracy after it. For example, the Great Binding Law established a system of checks and balances by which disputes among the tribes could be settled. The United States has a similar system that balances power among the different branches of government.

After listing the reasons why the colonies should rebel against the king, Jefferson finished with a phrase that justified many more democratic revolutions in the coming decades:

> A Prince whose character is thus marked by every act which may define a Tyrant, is unfit to be the ruler of a free people.

That Jefferson's words hold so much power today is a testament to his wisdom. He must have known that it would be a long time before any government treated all men as though they were created equal. But he knew his words would live longer than he would. They would give the new country a purpose. They gave all Americans a goal.

CHAPTER THREE

THE AMERICAN EXPERIMENT

The American Revolution for independence from Britain raged between 1775 and 1781. On July 4, 1776, the Second Continental Congress adopted the Declaration of Independence. In it, Thomas Jefferson had laid out a powerful vision of democracy. With the signing of the Treaty of Paris in 1783, the goal of independence was formally achieved. However, the task remained of figuring out how democracy in America would work. It would take the new nation more than a decade to find a sustainable way to implement democracy.

After the American Revolution, most Americans were scared to

George Washington was the commander in chief of the Continental army during the American Revolution. He became the first president of the United States in 1789.

give the government too much power—the king and Parliament had abused them for a long time. The founding fathers wanted to see how well America could work with as little government as possible. So they devised a system that gave Congress just enough power to accomplish what they felt was really needed. All other rights and powers were reserved for the individual states. Accordingly, they named the new country the United States of America.

Dividing Power

The thirteen original states could not agree on how the federal government should work. It took them years to resolve all their arguments. The small states argued that every state's voice should count equally, because they didn't want to get overshadowed. The big states countered that if every state had equal power, they should all pay equal taxes. Of course, the small states wouldn't agree to that. Moreover, the debate about slavery very nearly brought the whole process to a halt.

The Articles of Confederation

The agreement that the original states reached for America's first federal government was called the Articles of Confederation. It went through many revisions before all of the states were willing to give it a shot. However, by the time the articles were ratified, it was clear that they weren't going to work out.

Under the Articles of Confederation, the individual states were more like separate countries. Congress had very little power over them. In the absence of a strong federal government, several states had made their own treaties with other countries. Nine states had their own armies, and several had their own navies. Most of the states had their own currency, making exchange and trade among the states very difficult. Congress lacked the power to levy taxes, so it was always short of the money it needed for vital services. Within five years, the articles collapsed.

The first attempt to design a federal government had failed. But no one had ever attempted to establish a democracy on that scale before. The colonies

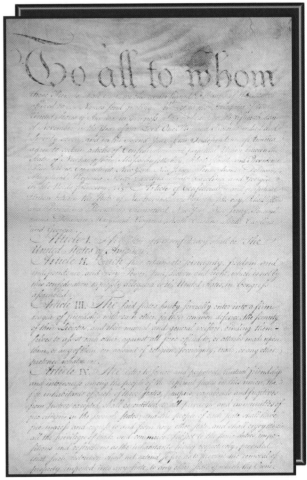

The Articles of Confederation had thirteen articles. Congress approved it on November 15, 1777. However, it wasn't enforced until it was ratified by Maryland on March 1, 1781. Refer to pages 56–57 for a partial transcription of the Articles of Confederation.

were much bigger than the Greek city-states that had inspired them. No one had ever dealt with the problems they were facing. Delegates learned their lesson quickly, though. If the states were

A DISPUTE OVERWHELMS THE ARTICLES OF CONFEDERATION

The final straw for the Articles of Confederation was a trade dispute between Maryland and Virginia. Under the articles, Congress did not have the power to regulate trade between the states.

The states didn't want Congress to be able to boss them around. But there was no higher power that could settle a disagreement between them and enforce its decision. The only hope was to find a workable compromise at the bargaining table. In September 1786, representatives from five states gathered in Maryland to try to settle the matter.

The discussion was long and tense. Finally, Alexander Hamilton, the delegate from New York, noted that the problem they faced was bigger than the matter at hand. Maybe they could solve the Maryland and Virginia problem, but other problems would arise soon enough. Without a system to solve them, the articles were not going to work. He proposed that the issue be put aside and a meeting be scheduled for the following spring. The meeting became the Constitutional Convention.

to be united, the federal government would have to be more powerful than they were. Each state would have to sacrifice some of its independence for the good of the whole.

On May 25, 1787, representatives from each state met in Philadelphia to address the shortcomings of the Articles of Confederation. This meeting, which lasted four grueling months, came to be known as the Constitutional Convention.

Alexander Hamilton *(center)* and George Washington *(right)* were delegates at the Constitutional Convention. They played important roles in supporting the Constitution after it was drafted. Thomas Jefferson *(left)* was on diplomatic assignment in Europe at the time of the convention. He objected to the large role that the Constitution granted to the federal government.

Once again, delegates turned to the philosophers for inspiration. They found their solution in the writings of the Baron de Montesquieu and John Locke. The secret was to divide the power so it wouldn't be invested in one place. Because Congress was the only federal body under the articles, the states had insisted that it be weak. To put so much control in one body would make it operate too much like a monarchy.

The Constitutional Convention

The matter of how to fairly represent all the states was a big stumbling block. The last time around, the debate had taken years. Now the Constitutional Convention was starting anew. Inevitably, the representation issue surfaced. It was clear that the federal government under the articles had been too weak. The new Congress was going to have the power to start wars, levy taxes, and negotiate treaties. So every state wanted to have as much power as it could. Thus, the whole debate began again.

Fortunately, this time the men at the convention found a solution quickly. They took a lesson from England's Parliament, which was split into two separate houses. America's legislature would also have two different houses. Both of them would need to approve a bill before it could become a law. They called the larger house the House of Representatives; they named the smaller the Senate. Representation for the House would be determined by a state's population. In the Senate, all states would be represented equally. That way, both the small and the large states would be happy.

Checks and Balances

The men at the convention devised a system that gave equal power to each of three separate branches of government. While individual states would have to sacrifice some of their freedom to federal power, none of the three branches of government could wield that power with impunity.

This was called a system of checks and balances. If any branch of the government overstepped its boundaries, the other two would be there to keep it in check. They could balance its power with their own. The first branch would be legislative, made up of representatives from every state, which would make laws. The second would be the executive, headed by a president, who would enforce the laws. The last would be the judicial, whose job it would be to interpret the laws.

The Issue of Slavery

There was another contentious issue facing the convention: slavery. The slave states wanted their slave populations to count toward their representation. That way, they'd have more power in the new Congress. But they didn't want their slaves to count toward their taxation. The nonslave states felt it should be the other way around.

If this had been the first time America was going down this road, the debate might have gone on for a very long time. It certainly may have gotten ugly. However, all of the delegates had a few things in common. They knew America needed a stronger federal government. They also knew that they couldn't spend as long arguing as they had when they were writing the Articles of Confederation. The problems would have to be solved soon, or democracy in America could fail.

Before long, the delegates reached a compromise. Slaves would be counted, for representation and taxation, but at only three-fifths of their true number. The Northern states were willing to agree to that because it meant more taxes for the treasury, which they wouldn't have to pay. But it didn't give the Southern states too much

This painting by Henry Hintermeister portrays George Washington, Benjamin Franklin, and other delegates of the Constitutional Convention signing the United States Constitution in 1787. Three of the delegates at the convention refused to sign the document. The painting is entitled *The Foundations of American Government*.

power in Congress. For the Southern states, the extra taxes seemed worth the extra voice in Congress.

There were some in the convention, including Benjamin Franklin, who passionately opposed slavery. But they knew that any attempt to outlaw or regulate slavery would alienate the Southern states. The Union was so young that it could not afford to create such a rift.

So even the antislavery delegates agreed to the three-fifths compromise and left it at that. They knew full well that the slavery question would have to be settled in some way later. But for the time being, they thought it was more important to keep the Union intact.

The Constitution

Between the checks and balances principle and the three-fifths compromise, most of the concerns about a stronger national government had been allayed. By September 1787, the convention was able to come up with a draft of the new Constitution that was acceptable to everyone present. The states were by then so eager

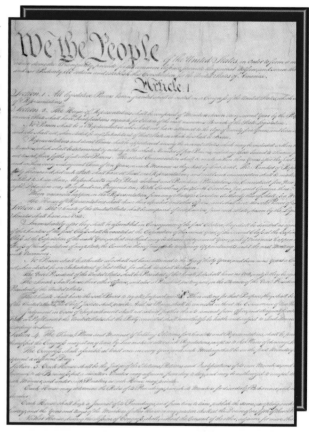

Every clause of the United States Constitution of 1787 came from the Articles of Confederation, the Northwest Ordinance, or state constitutions. Refer to page 57 for a partial transcription of the U.S. Constitution.

to move beyond the mess the Articles of Confederation had created that most of them put aside any problems they might have had with the new Constitution.

By June of the next year, the Constitution had been ratified, and the most complex system of government ever devised was set into motion. Except for the horrors of the Civil War, the system embodied by the Constitution has been successful enough to keep the Union not only intact but growing ever since.

Room to Grow

The framers' final bit of genius was to set out a clear system through which the Constitution could be changed. The men of the Constitutional Convention had a crucial bit of foresight. They knew that, no matter what, no system could be perfect. As history unfolded, someday it would need to be changed. They made it difficult, but possible, for the Constitution to change with the times. Since its creation, constitutional amendments have extended the right to vote to blacks, women, and eighteen- to twenty-year-olds. The Supreme Court has repeatedly reinterpreted the meaning of some of the Constitution's key passages, extending rights to groups that had previously been denied them. Even the Bill of Rights, the source of some of our most cherished rights as Americans, was not originally a part of the Constitution.

The framers of the Constitution gave democracy in America the room to grow and mature beyond their limited view. Had they not, America almost certainly would have collapsed long ago. Instead, its democracy has continued to grow and flower for more than 200 years.

CHAPTER FOUR

ELEMENTS OF DEMOCRACY

In the twentieth century, democracy spread around the globe. From countries to towns to clubs, each new democracy has conceived itself a little bit differently. Each one has found its own way of realizing "of the people, by the people, for the people." This plurality of visions has been a great benefit. It increases the number of ideas, good and bad, that exist about how to make democracy work. Like the Greek city-states, it has enabled the governments of today to learn from one another.

Nevertheless, there are a number of core principles that make a nation democratic. Among these are the ideas of the consent of the

Here, Arnold Schwarzenegger is campaigning to become governor of California in August 2003. He won a special election to replace Gray Davis, whom California voters determined should not finish his term in office.

governed, as described by Jefferson in the declaration, and a system of checks and balances among the executive, legislative, and judicial branches of governments. Other key features of democracies are free and fair elections, basic human rights, and the rule of law.

Free and Fair Elections

Elections are essential to representative democracy. However, the mere fact that a country holds elections does not make it a democracy. Many authoritarian governments hold elections to give the impression that they answer to the will of the people. However, these elections usually involve only candidates from a single party or only those of whom the government approves. Democratic elections must meet certain criteria. They should be competitive, periodic, inclusive, and definitive.

An election is considered to be competitive when it is open to opponents of the government. These opponents need to be free to speak and assemble in opposition to the government. Elections should be held at regular intervals. With the exception of judges, democratic elections should not place people in office for life. Voters are given periodic chances of selecting their leaders or representatives. Inclusive elections involve a large proportion of the adult population. An election that excludes a majority of the people cannot be said to be democratic. Consequently, during the era of apartheid when more than 80 percent of the population was denied the vote, South Africa was not a democracy. Elections are definitive when they determine the leaders of government, not just symbolic offices.

Voters in Arlington, Virginia, cast their ballots at enclosed voting booths on November 7, 2000. Voting by secret ballot has become an important hallmark of a democratic society. The practice was first used in what is now South Australia in the 1850s.

Voting in democratic elections is usually done by private ballots. In other words, voters cast their votes in secret. This minimizes the risk of voters being intimidated into voting for a particular candidate or issue. However, the counting of the votes and the management of the elections must be conducted as openly as possible to assure the citizens that the results are accurate.

This photograph shows computer analysts recounting the ballots at the Broward County Voting Equipment Center on November 8, 2000. The presidential election between George W. Bush and Al Gore in Florida was so close that election officials recounted the votes in several counties. The recount was closely monitored by media representatives, whose accounts were followed by the general public.

A common electoral feature in all democracies is that citizens are grouped into constituencies, or zones, such as a congressional district in the United States or a parliamentary constituency in the United Kingdom. However, most democracies have particular features or a combination of features that distinguishes them from the others. Nevertheless, there are two main types of electoral systems in the world: plurality elections and proportional elections. The plurality electoral system is often described as "winner takes all" because only the candidate who gets the most votes in the constituency is elected. This system is used in U.S. presidential, congressional, gubernatorial, and most local government elections. Under this system, a person can be elected to office with less than 50 percent of the votes. In some instances, where the election is between three or more candidates and none receives 50 percent of the votes, a second run-off election is held between the candidates with the two highest vote tallies.

In proportional elections, more than one candidate is elected to represent each constituency. The results are based on the proportion of the votes that a party or a candidate receives. A major advantage of this system is that minority groups, parties, and views have a better chance of being represented in the lawmaking bodies. Proportional representation is used in South Africa and in many western European democracies, including Germany, Finland, and Austria.

Basic Human Rights or Civil Liberties

The idea of everyone possessing certain basic rights is a cornerstone to modern democracies. Jefferson described these rights in the Declaration of Independence as being "unalienable." He meant that all human beings are entitled to these rights. Most democracies have their own list of basic human rights. However, the inalienable rights have been widely accepted to be freedom of speech, freedom of religion, freedom of assembly, and the right to equal protection under the law.

Freedom of speech is the right to express one's opinions or ideas without fear of government reprisals. When citizens fear voicing their opinions, governments are less responsive—and less accountable—to them. Freedom of the press is an important aspect of free speech. An independent press—one that is not controlled by the government—is essential to the spread of ideas. The press in a democracy informs the public about what the government and others are doing. By doing so, the press empowers citizens to make informed decisions.

Freedom of assembly is closely tied to freedom of speech. Citizens must be free to meet to discuss and debate ideas. Freedom of assembly allows citizens the right to form or join organizations such as political parties and interest groups. It also gives them the right to lead organized protests. This way, individual citizens can demonstrate the strength of their positions and can more effectively challenge the government.

The idea that no one should be required to practice a particular religion against his or her choosing is known as freedom of religion. It also means that no one should be punished for his or her religious beliefs or not practicing any religion at all. The United States follows a long-standing policy of separation of church and state. Accordingly, it has no national religion. Many other democratic countries, including Italy and Spain, have officially established or endorsed churches or religions. Nevertheless, their governments are required to protect religious minorities.

Equal protection under the law really means freedom from discrimination. In other words, the laws of a democratic nation should apply evenly and equally to, among others, rich and poor,

Supporters of President Bill Clinton cheer as his campaign train makes a stop in Royal Oak, Michigan, on its way to the Democratic National Convention in Chicago in 1996. The right to assembly applies not only to the rulers of a democracy, but also to their opponents.

ethnic and religious minorities, and opponents of the government. Equal protection under the law is also related to another major tenet of democratic societies: the rule of law.

The Rule of Law

The two main components of the rule of law are the notions of equal protection and due process. Equal protection dictates that no one should be above the law (receive special privileges) or below the law (subject to discrimination). The principle of due process of law holds that the rules and procedures that a democratic government follows in enforcing the laws should be clearly and publicly known and should not be exercised arbitrarily. Over time, a number of guarantees have been adopted as standards in democratic countries. These include the following:

Police should not break into and search a home without a court order showing good reason for the search.

No one should be arrested without explicit written charges specifying the suspected violation.

A person under arrest should be freed immediately if the court finds that the charge is unwarranted or the arrest is invalid. This doctrine is known as habeas corpus.

No one can be compelled to be a witness against himself or herself.

No one should be subject to "cruel and unusual" punishment, according to the laws and customs of the society.

A person under arrest is entitled to a speedy trial.

No one should be tried for the same crime twice. Therefore, a person who is acquitted of a crime can never be charged with the same crime again.

Antiwar demonstrators protest outside the Houses of Parliament in London on March 20, 2003. They were protesting against the start of the War on Iraq, in which England participated. The slogan "Not in my name," seen on the poster at left, is an example of a citizen denying his or her consent to the British government.

THE WEIGHTED BALLOT

One idea that is becoming more popular is called the weighted ballot. In most elections, the voters must choose the single candidate they like the most. But with a weighted ballot, they can rank as many candidates as they like, in order. This makes voters feel much more comfortable voting for a new or small political party. Since they can choose more than one candidate, they won't be wasting their chance to vote for someone with a better chance to win the election.

Another practice that's becoming more common is adding a "none of the above" option to ballots. That way, the voters who don't like any of the candidates aren't completely excluded from the political process.

Some of these guarantees date back as far as the Magna Carta of 1215. In the United States, many are embedded in the Bill of Rights and other constitutional amendments. The citizens depend on an independent judiciary to make sure that the executive and legislative branches of government do not compromise them.

CHAPTER FIVE

DEMOCRACY'S GROWING PAINS

Democracy is not a perfect political system. Throughout history, the reality has varied widely from the ideals at the core of democracy. The United States has become the standard bearer of modern democracy. Nevertheless, the country's history is riddled with practices that were blatantly undemocratic. Historically, democracy's guarantee of equal rights was belatedly extended to ethnic minorities and women. Today, more groups, including homosexuals, are making human rights claims in a quest for what they see as greater democracy. The meaning of democracy

This aerial view of the Washington Mall shows a section of the crowd at the Million Man March in Washington, D.C., on October 16, 1995. The Million Man March was one of the largest rallies in American history.

continues to evolve as democratic countries come to terms with these issues.

Slavery and the Breakdown of Democracy in America

Today, no American would consider a society in which slavery is legal as democratic. In fact, the United States equates democracy with freedom. However, for close to 100 years after the United States was founded as a democracy, slavery was legal throughout the country, especially in the South. Few people, including abolitionists who called for an end to slavery, questioned whether the United States was a democracy. Nevertheless, many people, including Abraham Lincoln, argued that slavery was inconsistent with the principles behind democracy.

Abraham Lincoln's election as president in 1860 precipitated a breakdown in American democracy. Pro-slavery Southern states refused to accept the anti-slavery Lincoln as president. Within months after Lincoln was inaugurated, eleven states seceded, or withdrew, from the Union. They formed the Confederate States of America. Lincoln was unprepared to see the nation fall apart. He clearly announced his intention to defend the Union with force if necessary. On April 12, 1861, Confederate forces launched a cannon attack on Fort Sumter in South Carolina. This action marked the start of the American Civil War, during which approximately 618,000 Americans died. Four years later, the Confederacy surrendered, and the nation became reunited.

The experience of the American Civil War provides an important lesson in democracy. In order to survive, democracies need to have a civic culture in which the losers accept the results of free and fair elections. By so doing, they allow for the smooth transition between administrations and continuity in the democracy.

On January 1, 1863, during the Civil War, Lincoln issued the Emancipation Proclamation, freeing the slaves within the Confederate States. This marked the beginning of the end of the institution of slavery in the United States. Slavery was ended after the Civil War, but the war had not been a cure-all.

The Emancipation Proclamation was the first major step by the federal government to bring black Americans within the folds of American democracy. Refer to page 57 for a partial transcription.

Lincoln used an undemocratic means—war—to achieve a democratic goal. He had bullied the South into submission, forcing it to free its slaves. But the entire plantation culture of the South was built on viewing blacks as less than human. Slaves were property, not people. It was going to take a long time for that perception to change.

Racial Discrimination

After the Civil War, Congress was still controlled by the Northern states. It passed three constitutional amendments to try to help blacks in America. The Thirteenth Amendment outlawed slavery. The Fourteenth Amendment guaranteed equal rights to all American citizens, regardless of their race. And the Fifteenth Amendment specifically guaranteed black men the right to vote.

The Southern states almost immediately started passing laws to undermine the new amendments. These were called the black codes, and they restricted the rights of blacks. Some of them forced blacks to pass various tests before they would be allowed to vote. Whites, of course, were exempt from the tests, not under the law, but in practice. They also passed segregation laws that made sure that whites and blacks were kept separate in public life. Blacks had to go to separate schools, stay in separate hotels, eat in separate restaurants, and ride in separate cars on trains.

In 1896, the United States Supreme Court ruled that it was con- stitutionally acceptable for states to require blacks and whites to use separate public facilities, as long as the facilities were roughly equal. The court's decision cleared the way for states—in both the North and the South—and the federal government to openly discriminate against African Americans. Segregation laws were rigidly enforced with both police measures and mob vio- lence. As a result, African Americans were for decades relegated to the status of second-class citizens whose basic human rights and were denied. Moreover, many states continued to set up obstacles to prevent African Americans from voting.

Virtually all aspects of life for African Americans were subject to these laws. They affected where African Americans lived, worked, and went to school—even where they were born and buried. Moreover, in every instance, the facilities provided for blacks were markedly inferior to those reserved for whites. The doctrine of separate but equal established by the Supreme Court's 1896 decision was in reality a myth.

The National Association for the Advancement of Colored People (NAACP) was formed in 1908 to fight segregation. After a series of legal challenges, the NAACP convinced the Supreme Court in the 1954 case of

Martin Luther King delivers his famous "I have a dream" speech during the March on Washington, D.C., on August 28, 1963.

Brown v. Board of Education that segregational laws were unconstitutional. This court victory helped spur the civil rights movement of the late 1950s and 1960s. Led by Dr. Martin Luther King, the movement successfully brought about a change in government policy and the public's attitude toward racial discrimination.

South African Apartheid

For much of the twentieth century, the doctrine of separate but equal was also in force in South Africa. It was called apartheid. Like its American counterpart, apartheid was concerned with the suppression of the black population. However, what made apartheid so striking was that more than 70 percent of the South African population was black. In addition, apartheid laws effectively denied all but the 15 percent white minority a voice in the nation's affairs. Under the Group Areas Act, citizens were segregated into white, black, and colored zones. Other laws restricted the movement of blacks.

During the apartheid era, South Africa had many of the trappings of democracy. Elections, although limited to the white minority, were freely and openly contested between various parties, and the transfer of power between administrations after elections was usually smooth. Also, South Africa was supported by many of the world's democracies, including the United States and the United Kingdom, for many years of the apartheid era.

After years of sustained struggle by the African National Congress and eventual pressure from the international community, South Africa abandoned its apartheid policies in 1994. Elections open to all South Africans were held that year. Nelson Mandela, the once jailed leader of the African National Congress, became president. Since then, South Africa has adopted a new constitution and has joined the ranks of the fully democratic societies.

The histories of other democracies are also filled with examples of large segments of the population, usually ethnic or religious minorities, being denied voting rights.

African National Congress leader and presidential candidate Nelson Mandela casts his vote in Inanda, South Africa, during the first all-race elections on April 27, 1994. He won the election. Only four years before, Mandela had been in prison serving a life sentence. He was imprisoned for nearly thirty years.

Women's Suffrage

In most of the world's older democracies, women were denied the right to vote long after democracy was established as the system of governance. In addition, women were also subject to other laws and customs that limited their rights to work, own property, publicly express their views, and enjoy an equal standing both at home and

Women suffragists picket in front of the White House in February 1917, demanding that women be given the right to vote. Many of the women who took part in this demonstration were arrested. Three years later, Congress passed the Nineteenth Amendment to the Constitution, guaranteeing women the right to vote.

in public. By the mid-nineteenth century, women in the United States and other Western countries began demanding voting and other rights. Led by Elizabeth Cady Stanton and Susan B. Anthony, among others, the women's suffrage movement in America agitated for voting right throughout the second half of the nineteenth century and the early twentieth century. The movement's efforts began to pay off in 1869, when the Wyoming Territory extended equal suffrage to women. One by one, other states began allowing women to vote. However, the federal government did not grant women's

CORPORATIONS AS THREATS TO DEMOCRACY

Not long before he died, President Lincoln expressed his concern about another threat he saw facing democracy. In a letter to a friend, he wrote the following:

> I see in the near future a crisis approaching that unnerves me and causes me to tremble for the safety of my country . . . corporations have been enthroned and an era of corruption in high places will follow . . . I feel at this moment more anxiety for the safety of my country than ever before, even in the midst of war.

Lincoln had worked for most of his life as a corporate lawyer. Even so, he had come to deeply distrust corporations. American corporations were becoming richer than they had ever been. Lincoln feared that they would use their wealth to unfairly influence the political process. And he was right. Over the next few decades, the U.S. government became incredibly corrupt. America became richer than it had ever been. The temptation for those in office to take bribes became too great. Fortunately, it was just a phase. Eventually, Congress passed a series of laws to address the problem, and the situation improved.

But today corporations wield more power over our politics than ever before. Many people believe their power has become so great as to undermine Lincoln's vision of "government of the people, by the people, for the people." What do you think?

suffrage until 1920. The first country to extend voting rights to women was New Zealand in 1893.

Other Current Issues in Democracy

In the United States, as well as in other democracies, the meaning and scope of democracy continue to be debated. The issue of gay rights has surfaced as the new frontier in basic human rights. Although homosexuals are not denied suffrage, many homosexual groups are pressing for the recognition of same-sex marriages. Only a few countries, such as the Netherlands and Belgium, allow such marriages.

In the United States, many interest groups are concerned about electronic voting. They fear that this new form of voting may be subjected to widespread fraud, thereby putting the results of elections in doubt.

According to Freedom House, a nonprofit organization that monitors freedom and democracies around the globe, there are about 120 electoral democracies in the world. This means there are more democracies than any other political systems. Although that number has remained relatively steady for some time, some countries have joined the ranks of democracies, while others have fallen from it. Democracy isn't guaranteed. It requires the active participation of citizens to make sure that those who govern do so with their consent.

TIMELINE

640 BC	The world's first known democratic government is established in the Greek city-state of Sparta.
508 BC	Democracy begins in Athens.
404 BC	Sparta conquers Athens, ending Athenian democracy.
338 BC	Philip of Macedon, the father of Alexander the Great, conquers all of Greece and ends Greek democracy.
AD 1215	King John of England is forced to sign the Magna Carta.
1400–1450	The Mohawk, Onandaga, Seneca, Oneida, and Cayuga Native Americans join together under the Great Binding Law. The world's longest-lasting democracy is established.
1762	The French philosopher Jean-Jacques Rousseau publishes *The Social Contract*, in which he further advances the cause of democracy.
1775	The American Revolution begins.
1776	The Continental Congress formally adopts Thomas Jefferson's Declaration of Independence.
1787	The U.S. Constitution is drafted.
1861–1865	The American Civil War is waged.
1863	President Abraham Lincoln issues the Emancipation Proclamation.
1893	New Zealand becomes the first country to grant women's suffrage.
1920	The Nineteenth Amendment is passed, guaranteeing women the right to vote in the United States.
1994	The first all-race election is held in South Africa.

PRIMARY SOURCE TRANSCRIPTIONS

Page 16: The Magna Carta (excerpted articles)

1. In the first place we have granted to God, and by this our present charter confirmed for us and our heirs forever that the English Church shall be free, and shall have her rights entire, and her liberties inviolate; and we will that it be thus observed; which is apparent from this that the freedom of elections, which is reckoned most important and very essential to the English Church, we, of our pure and unconstrained will, did grant, and did by our charter confirm and did obtain the ratification of the same from our lord, Pope Innocent III, before the quarrel arose between us and our barons: and this we will observe, and our will is that it be observed in good faith by our heirs forever. We have also granted to all freemen of our kingdom, for us and our heirs forever, all the underwritten liberties, to be had and held by them and their heirs, of us and our heirs forever.

12. No scutage not aid shall be imposed on our kingdom, unless by common counsel of our kingdom, except for ransoming our person, for making our eldest son a knight, and for once marrying our eldest daughter; and for these there shall not be levied more than a reasonable aid. In like manner it shall be done concerning aids from the city of London.

39. No freemen shall be taken or imprisoned or disseised or exiled or in any way destroyed, nor will we go upon him nor send upon him, except by the lawful judgment of his peers or by the law of the land.

Page 20: Declaration of Independence (excerpt)

We hold these truths to be self-evident, that all men are created equal, that they are endowed by their Creator with certain unalienable Rights, that among these are Life, Liberty and the pursuit of Happiness. —That to secure these rights, Governments are instituted among Men, deriving their just powers from the consent of the governed, —That whenever any Form of Government becomes destructive of these ends, it is the Right of the People to alter or to abolish it, and to institute new Government, laying its foundation on such principles and organizing its powers in such form, as to them shall seem most likely to effect their Safety and Happiness. Prudence, indeed, will dictate that Governments long established should not be changed for light and transient causes; and accordingly all experience hath shewn, that mankind are more disposed to suffer, while evils are sufferable, than to right themselves by abolishing the forms to which they are accustomed. But when a long train of abuses and usurpations, pursuing invariably the same Object evinces a design to reduce them under absolute Despotism, it is their right, it is their duty, to throw off such Government, and to provide new Guards for their future security.

Page 27: Articles of Confederation (excerpt)

I.
The Stile of this Confederacy shall be "The United States of America".

II.
Each state retains its sovereignty, freedom, and independence, and every power, jurisdiction, and right, which is not by this Confederation expressly delegated to the United States, in Congress assembled.

III.

The said States hereby severally enter into a firm league of friendship with each other, for their common defense, the security of their liberties, and their mutual and general welfare, binding themselves to assist each other, against all force offered to, or attacks made upon them, or any of them, on account of religion, sovereignty, trade, or any other pretense whatever.

Page 33: United States Constitution

We the People of the United States, in Order to form a more perfect Union, establish Justice, insure domestic Tranquility, provide for the common defence, promote the general Welfare, and secure the Blessings of Liberty to ourselves and our Posterity, do ordain and establish this Constitution for the United States of America.

Article. I.

Section 1.

All legislative Powers herein granted shall be vested in a Congress of the United States, which shall consist of a Senate and House of Representatives.

Article. II.

Section. 1.

Clause 1: The executive Power shall be vested in a President of the United States of America. He shall hold his Office during the Term of four Years, and, together with the Vice President, chosen for the same Term, be elected, as follows . . .

Article. III.

Section. 1.

The judicial Power of the United States, shall be vested in one supreme Court, and in such inferior Courts as the Congress may from time to time ordain and establish. The Judges, both of the supreme and inferior Courts, shall hold their Offices during good Behaviour, and shall, at stated Times, receive for their Services, a Compensation, which shall not be diminished during their Continuance in Office.

Page 47: Emancipation Proclamation (Excerpt)

Whereas on the 22nd day of September, A.D. 1862, a proclamation was issued by the President of the United States, containing, among other things, the following, to wit:

That on the 1st day of January, A.D. 1863, all persons held as slaves within any State or designated part of a State the people whereof shall then be in rebellion against the United States shall be then, thenceforward, and forever free; and the executive government of the United States, including the military and naval authority thereof, will recognize and maintain the freedom of such persons and will do no act or acts to repress such persons, or any of them, in any efforts they may make for their actual freedom.

GLOSSARY

amendment An addition made to a document at a later date.

blasphemy The act of attacking official or traditional beliefs.

body A governmental institution, such as the legislature or a court.

city-state A city and the villages that surround it. Roughly comparable to a county, except it had its own completely independent government.

constitution The document that defines the fundamental rules of a government.

federal Having to do with a whole country, as opposed to its individual states or territories.

legislation A document that establishes a law.

militaristic Fixated on military might or given to starting wars.

monarchy A system in which a king or queen holds absolute power over a nation.

oppress To use power to mistreat or keep down a person or group.

philosopher Someone who uses reason to analyze the way the world is and the way it should be.

representative democracy A system in which people elect delegates to speak for their interests in the government.

solidarity An act of unity with an oppressed person or group of people.

sustainable Able to be maintained indefinitely.

term limit A restriction on how a long a person is allowed to hold an office in his or her government. For example, no one can be U.S. president for more than eight consecutive years or two terms.

tyrant A ruler who uses absolute power unjustly to oppress his subjects.

unalienable Something that cannot be taken away, no matter what.

FOR MORE INFORMATION

The Martin Luther King, Jr., Papers Project at Stanford University
Cypress Hall, D Wing
Stanford University
Stanford, CA 94305-4146
(650) 723-2092
Web site: http://www.stanford.edu/group/King

U.S. National Archives and Records Administration
700 Pennsylvania Avenue NW
Washington, DC 20408
86-NARA-NARA (866) 272-6272
Web site: http://www.archives.gov/welcome/index.html

Voters for None of the Above
P.O. Box 26
Still River, MA 01467
Web site: http://www.nota.org

Web Sites

Due to the changing nature of Internet links, the Rosen Publishing Group, Inc., has developed an online list of Web sites related to the subject of this book. This site is updated regularly. Please use this link to access the list:

http://www.rosenlinks.com/psps/demo

FOR FURTHER READING

Favor, Lesli J. The Iroquois Constitution (Great American Political Documents). New York: Rosen Publishing Group, 2003.

Fradin, Dennis Brindell, and Michael McCurdy. The Signers: The 56 Stories Behind the Declaration of Independence. New York: Walker & Co., 2002.

Haskins, Jim. I Have a Dream. Brookfield, CT: Millbrook Press, 1994.

Ramsey, Sally. Quick and Easy Study Guide for the U.S. Constitution. Rock Hill, SC: Basic Educational Materials Publishers, 2000.

Richards, Kenneth G. The Gettysburg Address (Cornerstones of Freedom). San Francisco: Children's Book Press, 1992.

Rife, Douglas M. History Speaks: Gettysburg Address. Carthage, IL: Teaching and Learning Company, 1997.

BIBLIOGRAPHY

Arthur, John. Democracy: Theory and Practice. Belmont, CA: Wadsworth Publishing Company, 1992.

Church, Forrest. The American Creed: A Spiritual and Patriotic Primer. New York: St. Martin's Press, 2002.

King, Martin Luther, Jr. The Autobiography of Martin Luther King, Jr. New York: Warner Books, 2001.

O'Neil, James. The Origins and Development of Ancient Greek Democracy. Lanham, MD: Rowman & Littlefield Publishing, 2002.

Parker, A. C. The Constitution of the Five Nations, or the Iroquois Book of the Great Law. Oshweken, ON: Iroqrafts, 1991.

Simon, James. What Kind of Nation: Thomas Jefferson, John Marshall and the Epic Struggle to Create a United States. New York: Simon & Schuster, 2002.

Wills, Garry. Inventing America: Jefferson's Declaration of Independence. Boston: Mariner Books, 2002.

Wills, Garry. Lincoln at Gettysburg: The Words That Remade America. New York: Touchstone Books, 1993.

Page 7: Detail from *School of Athens* by Raphael, fresco, circa 1510. Located at Stanza della Segnatura, Vatican Palace in Italy.

Page 9: Undated photograph of the Pnyx. Located in Athens, Greece.

Page 12: *The Death of Socrates*, oil on canvas, 1787, by Jacques-Louis David. Housed at the Metropolitan Museum of Art in New York City.

Page 16: Handwritten copy of the Magna Carta, 1215. Housed at the National Archives and Records Administration in Washington, D.C.

Page 20: Original rough draft of the Declaration of Independence, 1776. Housed at the Library of Congress in Washington, D.C.

Page 22: *Congress Voting the Declaration of Independence*, engraving by Edward Savage, circa 1776. Housed at the Library of Congress in Washington, D.C.

Page 29: Nineteenth-century painting portraying George Washington in consultation with Thomas Jefferson and Alexander Hamilton. Created by Constantino Brumidi.

Page 32: *The Foundations of American Government*, painting by Henry Hintermeister. Photograph of painting housed at the Library of Congress Prints and Photographs Division in Washington, D.C.

Page 33: Signed copy of the United States Constitution, 1787. Housed at the National Archives and Records Administration in Washington, D.C.

Page 38: Photograph of election workers recounting presidential election ballots in Broward County, Florida. Taken by Alan Diaz on November 8, 2000. Courtesy of the Associated Press.

Page 47: Decorative lithograph of the Emancipation Proclamation, with portrait of Abraham Lincoln. Created around 1888. Housed at the Library of Congress Prints and Photographs Division in Washington, D.C.

Page 49: Photograph of Martin Luther King delivering the "I have a dream" speech in Washington, D.C.

Page 51: Photograph of Nelson Mandela voting in South Africa's first all-race elections. Taken by John Parkin on April 27, 1994.

Page 52: Photograph of women's rights activists picketing in front of the White House in February 1917. Housed at the Library of Congress Manuscript Division in Washington, D.C.

INDEX

PHOTO CREDITS

ABOUT THE AUTHOR

Bill Stites is a freelance writer from New York City.

Designer: Nelson Sá; **Editor:** Wayne Anderson;
Photo Researcher: Hillary Arnold